ANIMALITIES

Also by David Dodd Lee

The Coldest Winter on Earth
Orphan, Indiana
The Nervous Filaments
Sky Booths in the Breath Somewhere, the Ashbery Erasure Poems
Abrupt Rural
Arrow Pointing North
Wilderness (chapbook)
Downsides of Fish Culture

ANIMALITIES

David Dodd Lee

Four Way Books
Tribeca

Please direct all inquiries to:
Editorial Office
Four Way Books
POB 535, Village Station
New York, NY 10014
www.fourwaybooks.com

Library of Congress Cataloging-in-Publication Data

Lee, David Dodd.
[Poems. Selections]
Animalities / David Dodd Lee.
pages cm
ISBN 978-1-935536-48-2 (pbk. : alk. paper)
I. Title.
PS3562.E3383A6 2014
811'.54--dc23
2014011320

This book is manufactured in the United States of America and printed on acid-free paper.

Four Way Books is a not-for-profit literary press. We are grateful for the assistance
we receive from individual donors, public arts agencies, and private foundations.

NYSCA

This publication is made possible with public funds from the New York State Council on the Arts, a state agency.

[clmp]

We are a proud member of the Council of Literary Magazines and Presses.

Distributed by University Press of New England
One Court Street, Lebanon, NH 03766

CONTENTS

Our footprints are filling with pictures of water
—Allan Peterson, *Precarious*

The relations with animality are reversed; the beast is set free.
—Michel Foucault, *Madness and Civilization*

I'LL BE RIGHT WITH YOU

I flipped a coin into
a soda bottle and
wanted to believe in

something I had yet to
discover. Like when one
of my pills rolls across

the kitchen floor. You'd think
there was a great order
underlying all things.

INSTEAD OF NOTHING

Pearls, cannonballs, burnt cork . . . There's a trap door
that opens onto the sky, a ladder unfolding down to impulse

  and orange
juice. Protect me from what I want. I want you

to compliment me, my gray-indentations-in-white offset
some weekends by Hawaiian designs, the yellow of a

  pathological parakeet;
the blue of swirling sea currents, bipolar and without sleep

aids; this is Indiana. I can't breathe sometimes for the bats clogging
the attic's gable vents. I pay my rent and the ceiling

  uplifts my
dreams to irrelevancy, a basic understanding

I've developed because of the violence the moon inspires
upon my landlord and myself, each of us dying of our jobs.

SHE

Everything begins on the lost perimeter—
the deafening roar of crowds, in meetings, at close

proximity, the
recognition flows away from the deep water's fault.

It's a matter of processing it all. And the fragile edges
catch fire again. They're not far away—New Milford, the Mojave,

Staten Island—
as if a place could replace a name. As far as I know no one's

blinked. They're waiting for me. And the others wriggle
on home, the dust of my sleep increasing efficiency,

and metaphor.
The wind leafs through the pages on the music stand,

a dissonance. I almost *cried* last night, I make a small note. I was
navigating the handle of the big dipper toward Arcturus, to Virgo.

She was
that near to us, a distance apart. The stars would not solve for X.

A COUPLING

Because we are a brotherhood of women
and men suspended in a state of longing to

 cross over
and be something else, damn First Principles.

It's not exactly correct to say *For a long time I've wanted . . .*
How many actual minutes for example?

 My face
splits open like a hosta; we are a sisterhood

of bleeders. It's pretty male of me, she said,
wanting to interfere with my becoming . . .

REVIVAL

The outdoors jags along—it shifts its idea
  of itself
over the dishes, the stacks of books, interposes

with the fluidity of music, and consciousness—
  are you undressing
in the faces of such moonlit objects?

Furnishings, different in type, litter two porches.
  What's most true
won't even sit, or watch; it's devising a strategy

for decomposing your knees. Aesthetics is
  the invisible way the door's
pushed open, the air that constitutes everything

rivering your skin—it's also alive without asking . . .

"THE SOUL AS A SKIFF"

Can I talk now? Step away from the gate—
animals, some striped, stream across old

warehouse windows. I am approaching, with a bent key,
a steel door in East Williamsburg. No, my

hair is not hot. It smells of psychotropics. I see
a small cottage, maybe there's a tricycle

with red handlebars in front of it, boys and brown creepers
striding, laughing beyond the backlit mulberry groves,

wandering unborn in a goldenrod field. We'll never wake
up alone. Hands cuffed behind one's back. Edvard Munch's

face melts against the blood-black sky,
or he's shaking his head underwater while

the bathtub shares light; it burns her bones to blazing crystal.
I see a tiny white house—it's not the castle I live in,

nobody's shackled to the prow. It begins
raining in Wellesley. That was where I learned

my guardian angel is a liar. She called me Little Saint. She struck me
in the head with a wand made out of shallow pond reeds: first

I saw her feet naked, her legs, her wings folded. She said, My
breasts are not two fountains. Today my door facing the lake blows wide

open. A cardinal standing on my lawn is swallowing
an emotional rabbit. It is not upsetting. The sun is shining on Baugo Bay.

FUTURITY

Of course you've a story, kicked down the hall; terrible thing, a trip to Taco
Bell, where an ocean spills past the drive-thru window. Police lights waltz

  skyward, contrarily,
because we circle down from them. The roots of the oak trees reroute; small

voltages, bright groundwater (icicles stuffed into an elephant's mouth), an
exclusion of mind hanging in the sunshine like a vestigial landscape wiped clean

  of euphoria . . .
Everyone's face reminds me of a buried city, cars up on blocks leaning through

the slanted light (like jail cells), especially after shaking somebody's hand . . .
Gusts of blood cup the back of each eyeball as it un-sees us. Remember the

  flaming moon?
But the woman who says this recedes into hardwoods and moss. We

keep walking. Other peoples' waking, on paper, ruins the romance. We live, and this
becomes clear to me, boarding up my office. We can't help it. We can't help becoming

  a record
of somebody's witness ("deer flies had at her body"), perhaps passed around

like a virus, from person to person, until no one remembers. No one can
state it as such. No memory is graven. Retroactively, we are currently not happening.

ADULT FILMS

Forecast: pure chaos; they'll say it, and whether or not it be an
orderly destruction: here they all come. And what do we get for our trouble

  Mr. Milkstick
Century? Besides fracking? Brush the CEO's thinning hair nice and

even then 1) pull the plug toward the center of the room and
2) swing the plug-end around until it frightens the victim (a cover has

  been placed
over each available outlet). 3) Nonetheless, tap the **on** button. Let the bodies

"undulate" around the tied up sacrifice (paint the lenses of his
glasses bright pink). If that should fail to please most onlookers, focus

  your attention
on the now churning sea filling the room wall to wall. Bristle

your ugliest teeth. Use the trap door if you have to. Place a new
chair on the wood when the noise-level returns to a saunter . . .

THE STORY

Tobias Wolff wrote this story called
"Say Yes," and that kind of meaningful slick

stuck anyway;
one by one, to accumulate companion animals;

to colonize, interpolated with the spaces in the
landscape; Barthelme's "Margins":

the silver
bowl held a mixture of harmonious beans (You are

ultra-organized, artful; suffer egoism) . . . Hence the
handwriting all over the majority face; Carl leaning against

the architect's
building. One of the larger cats growled. She smelled good.

I didn't bother anyone. The brown shadow, the white sun
so delicate on the emerging human feelings. It was like

watering enthusiastic
patches of dampening hair. The hurricane remained outside

the city. Well you just poke at the inner mechanisms, Carl didn't
say, though I thought it. Then I folded the letter. The sidewalks

disappeared inside
the envelope. I held the stifled conversation in my pocket,

walked a block through snow, past Family Dollar, a boarded up church, the Men's Wearhouse. I walked quickly, the story in my hand.

UNGULATE IN THE PENTHOUSE OF THE WINTER TICK

It came insinuating itself up the stairway tower—
giant lonely great-hall where I trembled purposefully

between the
cries of atoms. You may surmise I have no idea what

I'm talking about. It's the slow heart. My cave in the fauna-
rich nursery, an australopith's tilted pelvis. I was never so

civilized; rather
looming up stairs like a moose thinking inwardly about

dark, deep water. Introversion is a celebration of being,
or else. Or else, I die smiling with you, sister. My white

skin under
hair, ridiculous narrative of the egg, until I pigment-out, sinking

into the cross-referenced strands of some evolutionary path,
too dumb to love it though. My color releases its secret . . .

CARNAGE

It's a side-swipe at best, but you anticipate the ricochets
and echoes, your reverberating head, *blunt force*, which are two words

    that flash
once in your mind like a word painting by Edward Ruscha.

One can't really say one was lucky to have lived. Though perhaps
it seems so to you, to me. There aren't any stars, just bodies blown out

    of consciousness
along with all consciousness; everything is abstract, retreating from form

(at least from this fixed perspective) . . . I almost want to say
I know what I want now, this trail of "no light" in all its remedial

    brilliance, unfollowable.
But I don't know, do I? I'm stuck with this carnage and joy.

REFLECTION IN A POOL OF WATER

The fan spins overhead. It always does, in
that room, a clipper. Fields burn and the crickets

  glow inside
them. Birth dates and death dates, a bottle resting

in the crotch of someone driving
under stars between burning buildings . . . I'm taking

  time-lapse photographs
and feeling the end of all things in the way the eventual green

is flung out in front of my face like a stop sign.
In other words, speaking does nothing. A car sails over

  a hill
but it's the plastic flapping in a barn window I notice,

certain of flight. I wash off the eyeshadow but the wind from
the fan doesn't bother the surface of my cup of coffee . . .

HALF SNOW, HALF RAIN

To liken everything to
substance. You're about to
live for this. Make the edges
out of habit such a thing you can't abide
because you were also mothered into being
while it snowed soundlessly for hours in nearby fields.

THE WHITE SEA

Spin the big wheel of weather. So it's seven
degrees. I could have sworn it was balmy and getting ready

  to storm
eight minutes ago. One definition of a slob is someone

who runs out to the street through a foot of snow in slippers
and a t-shirt to get the mail. And falls down. I close my eyes to

  the weather
and see black lemons floating on white water.

ESTRANGEMENT

The deer's face points downriver, marble-still, cold
eye into the wind, staring into the flashlight. Engine's shut off,

   snow on
the high banks. I slice her open on-site, organs spilling

into the water. Do the falling parts know that she's gone yet?
And the animal with its great black floor takes passage. She doesn't

   need to
worry anymore. The creek's stars quiver and absorb her. I light

my last cigarette. Barter trumps money in these woods.
Now her neck muscles are flowing out into the falling snow,

   hooves streaming
up into the gray machine . . . The eyes are deep set, polished already.

I'm still in awe. Later, I remove the head. She smells of wet rocks
and trees. I light a joint, rub the burn scars on my arm, remove

   the wire
frame for the gray fox, place the doe's head on the fleshing table.

I boil water. The body drains in the carport. I don't fear being away
from them anymore. It's quiet and the phone never rings.

SUFFERING THE UNATTAINABLE

Large sea turtles and some whales
will outlive us, water a manifestation of wind in

  another dimension.
I had to use the shovel to hack at the wood, had to grab

a hatchet, down deep in the hole. The oak pitched around
like a ship's mast, or I was no longer alive; perhaps I was yet

  to be
all over again, though I kept recalling your name. The verdurous roots.

DOCUMENTATION

No dextrin, from glue, and/or dandruff? Two silverfish exit, no food,
and not a single book left in the library. An earwig doesn't wait for

anything else
once uncovered, photosensitivity. Nothing feels concrete anymore.

The sunlight seems to exist without merit, a statue dissipating
under the roar of No End in Time . . . A silverfish will eat its own cast off

skin, intelligent.
I can see my sisters carrying a white end table out past the curb

like they are running away . . . like pigs running loose under two street
lamps, beautiful calves flexing, the joy of exhaling . . . As the meat of

such thinking
(or witness) I'm connecting the dots to each member—my mother

waving her vivid arms, my father honking his car horn at a light that won't
change. Light years are fictitious as history, but enable slow locomotion for

the large-jointed
vessel of the soul. Observation makes us trifoliate? I collect just a third

of my stuff, know later I will wash off the dead cells, rejoice
in relations but sign off on my piece of the monetary pie, crave protein.

RAYMOND CARVER

You left the milk out. Now it's ruined. I never moved
so quietly through such outlines, the rows of cedars

standing just
past the film of the screens. "What good's the use-by dating?"

My days at United Linens? The former coal miner flicked
his ash onto his plate with the chicken bones. This was

after the
armistice, the flaming peonies. More than a few stiff drinks. It

was summer. I had a skinned and gutted squirrel and a pot of
red potatoes. Wild asparagus. I wrote down and then drew

a line
through every job I'd ever quit after a single day. We would

appreciate it if you returned the store handbook. I can't find
my glasses again. I got out the lemon juice, the celery seed, the

big brown
knife I bought at an antique store in Yakima, Washington . . .

GARLIC

(New Year's Eve, 2012)

Desensitization to suicide, but not garlic; tests proved
the allergy. When I eat too much pesto (or go shopping)

  I develop
a low-grade fever. I like the suffering, knowing there will

come a time. I watch the frozen lake turn colors. Asphyxiation,
that's how J did it when I was in high school. Others followed,

  nine altogether.
I watched Les Blanc's *Garlic,* after number three,

at J's (no relation) in Twin Lake, who once made a video
of me ripping pages out of a phone book. Are you really

  that anxious?
Stimulation burns calories. Immediate light. Far away light.

YEAR NEVER

The wind actually did do such a thing. You just happened not to be watching—
daffodils in a next-door garden, rooms fading in the hospital. The Buick shining
junked under clouds in May . . .

What's mixed in the hand is peat, loess, a little hope.

It really is love.

I'd like to hold your hands—pretend I'm talking to both of you
at the same time. Sometimes the sun exhales on the Norway spruce in the front yard.

The curtains stop moving.

We might even identify this: Label A—for Almost Honest.

Sequestered, the morality of madness,
the conviction I'll smoke this first
cigarette in months, disappointment, no fire escape,

the uplifting resolve one's dependent on fate . . .

Despite everyone's dismay I'm not going to erase the even/odd pages in my book
   of hate.

Walking through the fir trees I realize I never say what I mean;

so talk back . . .

But how do you feel?

"Slipped in ignominy, the bones of a strangled killdeer, a playground. I will not share my toys.

Or *in process*, the soul-generated heat flows back and forth?

Her tits will feed multitudes.

A hockey puck."

Each time I pick a girl per her marigold, the leaning little piece of love blows the tension off my new pond's water surface. We're all part of the machine.

And this, from long before we ever met.

THE LESSON

The joy cannot continue,
cannot extinguish the fire in

  the bathtub,
the sirens roving from room to room

in the small house just down the hill
from the seven large houses, candles in

  every open
doorway. This is how you see in the dark, he says,

and he takes her hand in his hand, her hand
holding a yellow pencil, and he crosses words out.

FOR THE COUNTRY

(Happy Days Café, Wakarusa, Indiana)

We're buzzing and adrenal
with contempt,

then laughing—

a cork pops out of the life raft.

The cook wears a pea coat.

Northern-based diet, everything a smothering,
while the flickering reel
of a window

helps give life texture: a bird
poles a small
wagon under a traffic light . . .

at home she has finally gotten up

she can taste the air coming in through the screens

*

It's in the drink,
just north of Wakarusa,

sassafras in the joints,

the blur of test tubes where a tear might throb . . .

The usual contingencies and then this
tertiary

black light

her name in a cup,

the pine needles.

*

Elaborately complicated
by candlelight,

her fingertips stuck to my arm like sawdust.

Yes, though, I said, to the fresh
gleam of the wood and the yellow rope,

her spasmed anxiety,

the orange she's allowed to eat each day at 6 pm,

the time it takes
for the claw-footed tub to fill up.

*

"Hot Blooded" surges
on the radio

an unfortunate marriage of circumstance
and nostalgia

a nice haircut

a kiss on the cheek

crows on the phone lines like her little black shirts

*

The waitress's blood ran down the bright front window

He'd given her a photograph of "an ocean."

She took it, held it close

A mayonnaise jar full of weeds in some warm creek water

FLIP BOOK

Take the stubbed, slow man.
Glimpse him on the naked hill.
I found it lovely, the robber,

his sage face disproportionately
open like the many holes where
someone had blown up a house.

ROOM FOR RENT

The house is a cove, the house
is a cove, the house is a cove, the

   house is
a city, a stone's throw, a kindly

regurgitation, I'll admit
where have all the bellboys gone, off with

   the sluts
Yes we were in love with that kind of magic

Are you distant or something
The rain connects us with the water, the sadness

   is runoff
Can't you see the sun on the horizon bleeding

all over the surface of the lake
where the loons swim in it by moonlight still laughing

SUI GENERIS

It wasn't so much the tree frogs—
they were dead in the sewers hung up along

  the curbs—
or even the big platter of corned beef . . .

I picked up twenty knives before I found one heavy enough
because the heart's gnarled meat—you know this, right?

  The flowers
blooming along the windows in the elementary school

blistered like soft blouses . . .
Man looked at herself in a mirror and that was that

  The tape
looped back over and over again unlike the tracks of animals

ANTHROPOCENTRIC

Two rooms, six rooms, forty-five
rooms, and a man fishes for his

lighter in
his pocket. The cucumbers look so green

on the white plate. The wash sits in the sun,
clothes just out of the dryer, trees getting into the

people. That's
the idea, fluffed with air, how can anything feel

better. It can't, she says. Someone who doesn't like
the new neighbors starts writing things down. He's not going to get

over this.
One by one her buttons pop like firecrackers.

THE MUTE BUTTON

A pause is what fills the bottom
of the stairwell. The rest of the windows

   are paintings.
Like a train swallowing a beam of

shadowy air. Her story ends and mine
begins. I sigh, press "play." Usually no one

   is watching.
A cottonwood splits. Half of it silently

crashes to the ground. When the neighbors wake up
the yellow house across the street appears to be empty,

   swallows
flying in and out of the open windows.

NOT SEEN

Augustine said, for there is an attractiveness
in beautiful bodies; he mentions gold, "doth the

soul commit" a "fornication" . . . How
outsize are these personae—I never want to be

turned thusly in such studio light,
honest as a Doberman Pinscher, my flat-side

gleaming in a scurvy of tension. It smells
like something—you place the scorched pages in a carpet,

rolled up, everyone laughs—but the heart hurts—
you're lost in a George Saunders story.

There's so much grass, and images of grass, samples and
otherness, flopping under some warehouse window.

I get high-minded, or I find I'm in East Grand
Rapids, gravel and red plastic, some stuff glittering with pieces

of stone near a Ferris wheel
mural. I once was an innocence fishing—Stony Lake's

as good as anywhere—but you get the cellophane and straws
from drink boxes wandering up on the face. This is

what I mean about being a bigot of city and country—
whatever nabs you in the wrist. I find I can't help feeling

my discovery is of interest. Seen, they'd call it.
Notations on a screen, or maybe a little bit of wanting that,

which is not *the ideal*—in fact's cancellation
for the soul: dead privacy . . . Heard the cries

too often to just come back; Lexington, Kentucky, or east
of Eureka Springs, walking in a cave, raised deckle . . .

The water whooshes in the vat. The painting's of a bison—
she's smooth—her legs are human. She floats in time, ensnared.

FROM HAND TO MOUTH

I can't see you.
Semblance. I mean
The rain. The black

Rain. It's night you
Know, fingernails. Dragged.
And bitten off.

THE WHALES

The yellow-breasted bird is sinking into its mate—
black wings in the front yard. The cement mixer gushes like a thirsty

   silver wall
you hurl your body at; the waterline keeps rising. Ahab's still drowning

in this version, the newly renovated pond, windows unto
the basements and earth—our job is to save the whales. Dignity is awarded

   for silence.
If skin grew over your eyes, if you ballooned, if you found yourself

swimming under several small houses, 500-year-old white pines . . .
I went all the way back there, to the airplane kits, the old boys' restrooms,

   the guns
and coins in my father's office. A gray whale tossed one massive pectoral fin.

The houses stood their ground. I couldn't hear anything else though,
not through the wall, though someone was being ridden, harmed by love.

SAD FLOWERS

They're back-shot, black blood; we get the noon re-
port. It's divided into pieces—they aren't *out there.* They

  curve over
the wires. Hello, death in Africa, to me in my underwear.

Here's a blueprint of my pocket. When my face was wrapped
in muslin I could feel the dying animals, the places where they

  left salt
in my brain. Child, camel, things burned: what memories of

these will I bring with me out of the grave? Everyone has to
deal with lint. I pick the stuff off my aloe plant, it flows up

  out of
the baby's mouth and she's laughing like a dead jazz singer.

WHAT'S THE CAPITAL CITY OF ECUADOR?

I stopped speaking in my wolf-den voice by the time
I was in college. The administrator poked at his keyboard, a

classic ectomorph,
Are you seeing Disney characters anywhere? No,

I can't even name one. The literature on underground bats has them
as a food source for bad children, who if you ask me are the

only worthwhile
children. I'd watched *Jeremiah Johnson*. Closer to respect than can

be imagined, the furs I wore. Shared blood over snow is an
intimacy, write that on your little screen. There were TeeVees

on walls.
I first tried a pompadour—you can see this wasn't quite

working—but I wasn't finding my new "you." Number
of dependents? Roy Orbison. That made one . . .

WE HAD SIMPLY CROSSED OVER

It don't seem exactly humane . . . and so who is he scaring now?
That was the story, eye patch, like I'd been swallowing the exhaust

  coming out
of a Kawasaki motorcycle. Like a generator misfiring

in the basement, the rain outside, five half-smoked cigarettes. I'd
already burned myself on a baffle. Meanwhile at the Saint Louis Zoo,

  what the
hell were they crying about? The children simply ran

away from me, a pirate sweltering in the heat. I couldn't stop
playing at *Cutter and Bone*. But this was only my newest threshold,

  blind in
one eye now—how many lifetimes have you begged

let God forgive you? My family tree and how it is intertwined
with the Falstaff Brewing Corporation. I was standing with friends

  in front
of an Aldabra tortoise. *I'll pay for dinner,* I said.

The tortoise was being fed some lettuce. Normally I love a zoo. I
needed shade. It still felt like I was swaying in that fucking arch.

PROCEDURAL

... the object must be eliminated from the picture.
—Piet Mondrian

The thing is, I don't want to explain it to you, nor should we
celebrate our great representational failures: You're just

so obviously
not Kazimir Malevich . . . Here in deep space, I'm wearing

a robe that opens in back. That's when my face seems
most to misrepresent me. Go on, I relent, I've

got insurance,
and soon I'm inhabited. My theory about explication

being reductive requires no further defense. Someone's
delighted. The questioning swarm beats a path through the

backyards
of decency. Just look at these marks. Your three-dimensionality

should begin to reverberate. The red and blue bars don't lock us out.
The viewer has become the figure. The doctor hands me a bright

color printout.
Overlaid arrows indicate the presence of diverticulum . . .

KEITH MOON

It's not hovering. The Bible that cracks open
is glue, integument, tree bark; a book full of pain and

   death. Insecurity.
Stir the plaster of Paris, or whatever it's fucking called,

until it comes. You're a presence from your hair follicles
down to your anus. Thank God you learned to

   play drums
while the others were mapping out their careers.

TCHAIKOVSKY SINGS THE MORNING

(December 15, 2012)

Winter's not arrived this December . . . In *The Nutcracker*
Clara's prince leads her to snow, and maybe the nightmare of

  a squarer
face, a guillotine, her muscles tingling in her legs . . . the shooter looks

through all the school's windows the night before. He bleeds back to his
awful birth. Why is there something instead of nothing? I notice this in the

  pond ice,
a web of cracks, a walleye pushing through the front of my face so that

all I can see from the shore is my breath in small bursts. There's veganism,
my father's stroke; my refusals, my newfound flexibility;

  drizzle rising
into the sky until it doesn't freeze, steam rising off the one bald

head visible on CNN in the December heat of the press conference.
The nutcracker is an expert at cracking nuts. His eyes spiral until the shooter's

  gun clatters
to the floor. Clara takes the little hero-prince to bed before embarking on

an acid trip . . . I was six once. From my closet, a man with a walrus mustache,
smoke coming out of his mouth due to the hot meat he was chewing,

  kept smiling
at me until I closed the door. It snowed for eight days without stopping.

UNNAMEABLE YOU

I've got a bumper sticker I'd like to whitewash
onto your face, maybe there near the tab for Birth

Date, economics,
all the sliced cling peaches called citizenry. Tell me

(I'm wearing new contacts) Detective . . .
(I have to lower a pocket flap) Detective

Muncie. What
are they reading on the moon these days? I don't think this glass

has been properly cleaned, my goodness!
He had these accents in his hair, Poor Britney, he screamed,

getting pixelated,
like with a big blue fishing lure or smart phone streaming out of his

emoting face, the canyons in our country resonating with the cries
of tourists happily riding asses, What else are you thinking

about—immortality,
fame? Trying to (crying) grow a beard, dependable vacuum cleaners,

the reanimation of Eric Heckel, and I thought, all right, I can understand
that kind of passion, arrows spilling from the sky, bloodied, grave, naïve . . .

CONSPIRACY THEORY

Kenneth, what is the frequency?

I wish you calm a boat rising in winter
snow ice the remaining leaves late blackbirds

Footage a
word we should bury but he was knocked over

the hood of a Studebaker with a stick, dear
Dan Rather, into the studio, past makeup

(I guess),
and Donald Barthelme, scratching his chin hairs,

thinking Grand Canyon My Jock Strap Flies Proudly
From My Old Impala Antenna the last thing we need is

more black
and white footage please please I beg make a snowball

AN EXPLANATION

How can I say I live where you live.
I'm brought down from the sky. I'm intimate with

  the air
that sweeps over the other terrestrial faces. We're all eating the same

chance to be forgotten, midges we'll never swat. I float down to you
where the oxygen streams, we get in the bed, we're animals behaving . . .

  I don't
know how long the other life took. The tadpole, everyone's child,

loses its tail and the head bulges out of the water
and the eyes say I'm not afraid to die. I want to go home.

VOCATION

Front-loaded,
every
day back once again

Reminds me of the
hotel rooms—
you know the hotel rooms—

you sit on your bed with a smile strapped to your face

a farm pig . . .

perhaps wondering about sex

or bedbugs

But let's get ourselves far far away from all that

*

What's the secret to sitting down?

(owning a stopwatch)

I still possess the ability to recognize the original fetal face in an adult
  human being . . .

What's it mean to be wise, or right?

WE STAY HERE

I did it so I would know too much, like
a trash compactor. You've got to unlearn these

   things, panting
over his pancakes, sex-smell in his chest hair, a cool

breeze swirling in through the open window. A
painting of two nudes carrying a deer on a pole

   rattled on
the wall. Right then I could imagine our backbones,

our postures without flesh, spines bowed sitting up, or
supine on a table, the scraping tools of the scientists,

   the fact
that we are solid after all, like a grocery cart.

VAUDEVILLIAN

I remember children drifting out into the sweet-smelling orchard
of perfect apples, sunbeams that then evaporated;

They're gone,
someone said. They were dead. They'd become tarpaper. I don't know

how to get out of these grief circles . . . I stand in the kitchen,
imagine the faces of ticks and of flies: how there's something blunt

in them.
I overhear them talking to one another, fly to fly, father

to the child he never was. Like one of the faceless, burned,
laughing without expression. Is that the 1970s "you" looking back at

yourself in
the sliding glass door? The staircase painted white still looks like a waterfall.

GLOSSED: THE SPIRIT SAYS *COME BACK HERE*

I can't roam this piece of hard earth—I can,
but I am so not going anywhere—better to sit myself down, no revolutions . . .

Evanescing into, anyway, rising slipknots . . .

I am a chain of astral fog
My lungs and even my arms feel stuffed with the brightness of air-conditioning

I can't make any sentences, I'm unable to think to myself, because the
words feel like they floated away two months ago

Explain this separation—but at least I'm no longer sinking, shells of lead
growing around the thing I've been humoring inside, subtle

Three inch holes in the sod, I'm going to inter myself

Ten million pages fly backwards and the light does shift; it all goes black

I get five miles or so way up past the clouds until I disappear from where
I'm standing but when I look down again I see someone standing there and
  then my brain erases

THE IMPOSSIBILITY OF LOVING MANKIND AS A WHOLE

They test the emergency broadcast sirens on Saturday,
close down the beer coolers on Sunday. Paradise

thunders. The
skins of the half-flaming apples leak serpents, and a Canada goose

meets two people on a path. There isn't enough shame
to go around. Once-removed from the love of God, the goose is

simply shot.
A truck graced with a confederate flag ferments in a heat wave;

deer in a pile, hooves separated; there's no divinity like making
a sale, cleaning the hills to a burnished luster. This other wasn't

for meat—
dead wings on the water—or sport. Goose as fragment of the benevolent

imagination of oceans, lord of the sea-skies—we pray. For the bird,
not man. An animal's not an immanence merely by virtue of scripture . . .

NOTES

"Not Seen" references Werner Herzog's *Cave of Forgotten Dreams*.

"Sad Flowers" was influenced by the Howard Hodgkin painting entitled "Sad Flowers."

Robert Creeley wrote the last line of "Vocation."

The title "The Impossibility of Loving Mankind as a Whole," comes from Tolstoy by way of Andrei Tarkovsky in his film *Solaris*.

Also, prompts here supplied by Donald Sultan ("The White Sea"), Bruce Nauman ("From Hand to Mouth"), William Bronk, Giorgio Agamben, and Jean Francois Lyotard.

Thank yous go out to Martha Rhodes and Ryan Murphy for making this book possible. Thank you for your support: Russell Thorburn, John Walson, Charmi Keranen, Nancy Botkin and Elaine Roth. Thank you to the journals who published poems that appear in *Animalities*. This book is dedicated to my mother, in memory.

ACKNOWLEDGMENTS

Poems in *Animalities* have appeared in:

Barn Owl Review, Construction, diode, Elimae, The Fiddleback, Guernica, The Laurel Review, The Offending Adam, The Portland Review, and *Superstition Review.*

David Dodd Lee is the author of eight previous books of poems, including *The Coldest Winter on Earth* (Marick Press, 2012). His fourth book, *Sky Booths in the Breath Somewhere, the Ashbery Erasure Poems* (BlazeVox, 2010), taught him how to write the poems in his next books: *The Nervous Filaments* (Four Way Books, 2010) and *Orphan, Indiana* (University of Akron Press, 2010). He is the editor of two poetry / fiction anthologies: *Shade 2004 & 2006* (Four Way Books) and *The Other Life: the Selected Poems of Herbert Scott* (Carnegie Mellon, 2010). His poems have appeared in *Court Green, Denver Quarterly, Field, Jacket, The Nation, Nerve*, and in many other places. He is also a visual artist, writes and publishes fiction, publishes chapbooks and full-length titles as editor-in-chief of 42 Miles Press, and teaches classes in poetry, publishing, art history, and the art of collage at Indiana University South Bend, where he is assistant professor of English. He lives in Osceola, east of South Bend, where he kayaks and fishes on Baugo Bay.